OURAY

JACK BENHAM

1976

ISBN: 0-941026-01-9

OURAY, COLORADO
BEAR CREEK PUBLISHING CO.
514 MAIN STREET
81427

THE AUTHOR

Jack Benham has been a competent mining geologist for many years and his searches for uranium have taken him to many of the mining camps of the western U.S., enabling him to pursue his interest in western history. He is an insatiable explorer of the back trails, the hidden valleys and those collectible items of history that make for footprints in the sands of Colorado's past. Benham's Colorado roots are deep. Born in Illinois, he first moved to Colorado in the late twenties and completed his education in Illinois upon the death of one parent. Returning to Colorado after World War II, he attended old Ft. Lewis College at Hesperus, later moving on to Boulder and the University. He received degrees from Colorado State University and the University of Idaho.

I first knew Jack Benham while we were both students at the University of Colorado in the late 1940's when he and his wife lived in the old gold mining camps of Crisman and Salina. As a mountain carrier for the Denver Post and the Boulder Daily Camera, he made daily trips to Gold Hill, Jimtown, Nederland and other camps. A quote from Benham refers to the motor route as "110 miles of the longest, crookedest, highest, dustiest, chuck hole-iest, and least renumerative paper route in the state of Colorado".

He has continued his route, but for different reasons and in different places all over the west. Now Jack and Sadie Benham live in Ouray and it is only right this his first book on Colorado history is about that city. This book, a factual history of Ouray in the eyes of Benham, has sixty pages of pictures and facts that have been gleaned from many hard to find sources. We can all be thankful that he is a versatile writer, and as said of Dave Day on his death, "his sole purpose in life was driving nails of truth with the proper hammer." We look forward to more Colorado history from Jack Benham.

BILL LINDSEY, Secretary-Manager
Colorado Press Association

Cover by Richard Wagner, Telluride's nationally known artist. Mr. Wagner's paintings may be seen in the collections of the Library of Congress, Denver Art Museum, University of Colorado, Dartmouth College, Rochester Museum and others. His work has been shown at The Museum of Modern Art, Pennsylvania Academy, Carnegie Institute, Joselyn Art Museum, Colorado Springs Fine Arts Center, and many more.

CONTENTS

CHAPTER I

CHAPTER II

CHAPTER III

CHAPTER IV

CHAPTER V

Early sketch of Bear Creek Falls and Ouray with Otto Mears' toll gate and hostel that appeared in 1888 publication, Picturesque California, by John Muir. The prominent building in center of town is the Beaumont Hotel. *(Denver Public Library, Western History Department)*

ACKNOWLEDGMENTS

The Western History Department of the Denver Public Library and the State Historical Society of Colorado Library contributed the majority of the photographs. Mr. William Stark of Ouray kindly furnished the photograph of the elk in front of the Ouray Elks Lodge. The libraries of The State Historical Society of Colorado in Denver and the Walsh Public Library in Ouray assisted in supplying reference material. The writer thanks the staffs of the above named organizations for their cooperation. The writer also wishes to thank Kay Wilcox, Research Librarian, and Eleanor M. Gehres, Head, Western History Department, Denver Public Library, for their research assistance.

Special thanks also go to Richard Wagner, a friend since our student days at CU, for his cover sketch of the Beaumont Hotel and narrow gauge caboose.

INTRODUCTION

Ouray, called Uncompahgre City by its early settlers in 1875, is located at the confluence of Canyon Creek and the Uncompahgre River, and is encompassed by near 13,000 foot mountain peaks. Uncompahgre is a Ute word meaning warm springs or reddish waters and refers to the numerous hot springs that abound in the area. The town of Ouray was named for the chief of the Uncompahgre Utes who lived in the valley of the Gunnison and Uncompahgre Rivers. Chief Ouray befriended the settlers and is credited with preventing Indian uprisings in western Colorado. The Utes, joined in a loose confederation of seven bands, were the oldest continuous residents of Colorado. Their presence discouraged the exploration of southwestern Colorado by the Europeans, the first conflict with the Spanish occurring in 1637. In 1765 Juan Rivera made the first recorded expedition into the San Juan Mountains from Santa Fe, eventually reaching Delta, Colorado. In 1776 Fathers Escalante and Dominguez, traveling from Santa Fe to Utah, crossed the Uncompahgre River just south of Montrose. The Mountain Men invaded the western lands of the Utes in the early 1800's. In 1828 Antoine Robidoux built a trading post, the first in the southern portion of the Intermontane Corridor and the second west of the Continental Divide, near the present site of Delta, thereby influencing other Americans to develop the Great American West.[1] The well-traveled Cochetopa Pass route of the Spanish Trail connecting Santa Fe to California, passed within less than forty miles of the present site of Ouray. Although there are no records to indicate the Spanish or Mountain Men ever ventured up the Uncompahgre River to the present site of Ouray, it is very likely that they did in their search for gold and furs. Perhaps the early discoverer purposely chose not to reveal the site of such abundance and beauty.

Ouray.

Chief Ouray, chief of the Tabeguache or Uncompahgre Utes. About 1876. Handwriting is reported to be his own. *(Library, The State Historical Society of Colorado)*

OURAY

CHAPTER I

Gus Begole . . . Settlement of Ouray . . . Los Pinos Ute Agency . . . Fort Crawford . . . Sidney Jocknick . . . Otto Mears and Saguache to Lake Fork Toll Road . . . First mail to Ouray . . . Ladies hats and black powder . . . Ouray becomes incorporated . . . Chief Ouray and Chipeta . . . Lake Fork and Ouray Toll Road . . . Saguache . . . Telephone and telegraph service . . . Early day smelters . . . Volunteer fire department . . . Thatcher Brothers and the Miners and Merchants Bank . . . Citizens State Bank.

Gus Begole and Jack Echols, two prospectors from the Silverton area, are credited as being the first settlers in Ouray. Like many of the early prospectors, they had ventured away from the established mines along the Los Animas River and its headwaters and were searching for silver and gold in the Uncompahgre area. In 1875 they found an outcrop of closely-spaced, parallel veins, suggesting row crops, and they consequently named the claims the Mineral Farm group. The word spread rapidly, others followed, and numerous claims were staked within the next few months. Cabins were built and a few hardy settlers remained for the winter.

In the meantime in Washington, a decision had been made during the summer of 1875 to move the Los Pinos Ute Agency from the Cochetopa area to the Uncompahgre Valley. The Uncompahgre Agency was established near the present site of Colona by late fall and the Military Cantonment named Fort Crawford, was built four miles north. Sidney Jocknick was a cowboy at the Cow Creek cow camp and has recorded many early incidents. Otto Mears had recently completed the Saguache to Lake Fork of the Gunnison toll road into Lake City over which the Barlow and Sanderson Stage Line made tri-weekly runs. Mears was awarded the contract to deliver the mail from the Lake City to the Agency, a distance of seventy miles. Ouray and the miners initially used the Agency as a dispatch and receiving station for mail. An old prospector, Stewart Daniels, who had once been employed by the Hudson Bay Fur Company, suggested to Mears that he use dogs in the winter, "Esquimo fashion".[2] Mears immediately accepted the proposition and appointed Daniels a carrier. Mears used a toboggan drawn by dogs with a man alongside on "Norwegian shoes", the equivalent of present day wide skiis. No problems arose in the winter except from the few people who remained in Ouray and received their staples and other supplies by mail. It

Ft. Crawford on November 18, 1886. Bakery on right had capacity of 300 loaves. Building later moved, remodeled and is presently standing east of the highway. Hospital is on far left and guard house with cannon is in center. *(Library, The State Historical Society of Colorado. Photo by T.M. McKee)*

Ouray, Colorado in 1886. The Beaumont is under construction. Cascade Falls can be seen flowing on the left and peaks of Amphitheater tower out of view on the right. *(Library, The State Historical Society of Colorado.)*

seems that some of the ladies also ordered hats and dry goods. The man and the dogs would sit on the toboggan occasionally to get their feet and hind ends out of the snowbanks, smashing everything so that black powder, tobacco, coffee, sugar and ladies' hats would get all scrambled together. The ladies of Ouray complained to the Department about the damage to their hats and it was decided that mail delivered by toboggan and snowshoes would henceforth not include items such as ladies' hats and general supplies. By the spring of 1876 the snow became so deep that neither dogs nor snowshoes could be used, and the carriers quit. To avoid being assessed a penalty for non-delivery, Otto Mears himself carried the mail. Due to the deep, soft snow, it took three difficult days to reach the Uncompahgre Valley from Lake City.

Ouray grew rapidly and by the end of 1876, the year the town was incorporated, it had a population of 400 with 214 dwellings, four general stores, two sash-and-door factories, two blacksmith shops, one sawmill, one ore sampling works, a schoolhouse with forty-three students, two hotels, and a U.S. post office.[3] A wagon road was incorporated from Ouray to connect with the Lake Fork of the Gunnison road at Indian Creek the same year. This road, the Lake Fork and Ouray Toll Road, was built by Otto Mears and provided Ouray with good access to Saguache, 130 miles, the closest supply center. The toll gate was on Skyrocket Creek, north of the present day swimming pool. Due to the fear of the Utes uprising in the Uncompahgre Valley, a militia company was formed to protect the town. This never became necessary, and its only claim to fame was its participation in early day parades. The Utes were frequent visitors to the new settlement where they raced horses, gambled and traded. On several occasions Chief Ouray, who was often accompanied by his wife, Chipeta, was called on to serve as moderator in arguments between the whites and Indians. The most serious problems were caused by the men of the town selling liquor to the braves and taking their women. Ouray incorporated a waterworks in 1877 and telephone lines were established between Ouray, Lake City, Mineral Point, and Silverton the following year. The San Juan Telegraph Company was also formed and remained in service until the Western Union came to Ouray with the railroad in 1887. The Munn Brothers Sampling Works was one of Ouray's first businesses and stood west of the present day Circle M Motel. By 1879 there were three small smelters with a total daily capacity of seventy-two tons within three miles of town. The Presbyterian Church built by pioneer missionary, Reverend George M. Darley, was the first church in Ouray and the second on the western slope. A volunteer

T. Y. Bradshaw house can be seen next to Courthouse. Later owned by Judge Icke.

(Denver Public Library, Western History Department)

Louis King house, reportedly built in late 1870's. House is still standing on 7th Ave. between 3rd and 4th Streets. The back of the Dixon house can be seen in far left. *(Denver Public Library, Western Historical Department)*

fire department had been formed as the city grew and its members with their colorful uniforms were, in later years, popular in parades and contests. The department consisted of a hose company and a hook and ladder company. Thanksgiving Day and the Fourth of July were set aside for their celebrations. Ouray had its Magnolia Band and numerous patriotic, social, and secret orders. Crofutt stated in his 1885 Guide to Colorado that "the secret orders are so numerous and varied that few citizens think of keeping a secret."

One of the leading banks of the area, The Miners and Merchants Bank, was formed in 1878 by the Thatcher brothers of Pueblo, who owned a chain of banks in the major mining districts of the state. The Citizens State Bank was organized in 1913, a few years before the Thatcher family closed their bank to concentrate their efforts on their business in Pueblo. The bank moved to a corner room in the Beaumont Hotel when it was completed. The name Thatcher Brothers, can be easily read in early photographs. The brothers are reported to have advanced the $600 thousand necessary to drive the Revenue tunnel from the portal location at Sneffels, a distance of 7400 feet to intersect the rich Virginius vein at depth.[4] The Citizens State Bank had excellent directors and it was the only bank in Ouray, San Juan, and San Miguel Counties that did not close its doors during the depression years. At the present date it serves customers in a four county area.

Ouray Fire Department in their Fourth of July finery ... about 1906. *(Denver Public Library, Western History Department)*

CHAPTER II

By late 1877 the Denver and Rio Grande Railway had laid tracks
westward as far as Alamosa. The distance from Ouray was 200
miles. The Barlow and Sanderson Stage Line made passenger
connections to all major railway centers. Their red Concord
coaches with four or six horses were a familiar sight to the San
Juan traveler. During winter months sleighs were often used if
the snow-packed trails would support the horses' weight. In 1878
Barlow retired and the official name of the company was shor-
tened to J. L. Sanderson and Company. However, the former
name continued in common usage and in the September 5, 1879
edition of the Solid Muldoon an ad by the Barlow and Sanderson
Stage Line states that the running time between Ouray and
Alamosa via Saguache was thirty-four hours. In 1884 the line was
sold to the Colorado and Wyoming Stage, Mail and Express Company. Due to the continued expansion of the railways, their runs
soon became confined to the remote mountain areas, such as
Ouray and Silverton.[5]

Due to the onerous and slow travel conditions in the Ouray
area, many small post offices were established. Five miles north
of town the post office, Ash, served the 200 or so miners and their
families at the Bachelor and Calliope mines. A round trip to town
required half a day. One post office near Ouray was the highest in
the United States. This post office and store was at the Virginius
mine camp, 12,500 feet in elevation. The post office was later
moved to Sneffels upon completion of the Revenue tunnel in 1895.
Mail was transported at one time or another by all possible
means; dog sleds, stage coaches, pack teams, horseback, snow
shoes, skiis, and sledges, all were used. Snow slides killed more
than one carrier during the winter months. In the Silverton area,
Ben Harwood packed mail on snowshoes for several winters from
the foot of Grassy Hills over the Continental Divide to How-
ardsville and Silverton, at the same time carrying from fifty to
eighty pounds of beef or supplies to drop off at the Highland
Mary mine.[6] By 1881 mail was delivered from Ouray to Mineral
Point via Poughkeepsie, ten miles and back, three times a week.
Montrose mail trips were daily, by coach and four. Before the end

Burros packed for the mountains, Ouray, Colorado. *(Library, The State Historical Society of Colorado. Photo by William H. Jackson)*

Heavily laden with ore sacks, a burro pack train nears home after a trip to one of the mines in the high country. *(Denver Public Library, Western History Department)*

Ouray's lumber yard and departing lumber train. *(Denver Public Library, Western History Department)*

Radium Springs Park north of town with goldfish ponds and baseball park in background, 1910-1920's. *(Denver Public Library, Western History Department. Photo by G. L. Bean)*

of 1884 mail was also delivered from Ouray to Ironton, Red Mountain, Chattanooga, and Silverton six times weekly by a Concord coach and four. Mt. Sneffels mail was delivered three times a week.[7]

Ouray's first newspaper, The Ouray Times, was published in June 1877 and continued through mid-1886, when it became The Ouray Budget. It was a Republican paper and when David Frakes Day and his friend, Gerald Letcher, needed capital in 1879 to purchase and move a newspaper plant from Lake City to Ouray, they raised money from the Democrats.[8] Day named his paper "The Solid Muldoon" in esteem for a New York City fight promoter who was popularized by a song of the time as being an honest man. The Solid Muldoon became an instant success in all the mining camps of the San Juans, Colorado, and the western mining states. Day's spicy wit was in keeping with the rough and tumble times of the early San Juan camps. One famous example appeared in his paper, noting the Editor, while wondering through a country churchyard, had discovered the following inscription on a tombstone:[9]

"Here lies the bones of poor old Charlotte,
Born a virgin but died a harlot;
For eighteen years she preserved her virginity,
A damn good record for this vicinity."

His editorials were sharp, witty, risque, and quotable. He was absolutely fearless in scrapping for what he believed was right. This was not a new approach for the man, as he had been a Union soldier at the age of fourteen, a chief of scouts for the 17th Army Corps at the age of seventeen, was captured three times, escaping a like number, wounded four times, awarded the Medal of Honor for his service at Vicksburg, and discharged with almost four years service at the age of nineteen. He had no use for pompous, officious bureaucrats or politicians, deceptive mine promoters, and blow-hards in general. He was not above provoking a harsh rebuke from a wounded adversary through his witty sarcasm. At one period of time, he had forty-two libel suits pending against him. Needless to say, he didn't pay out one cent in judgements. He toured Europe in the late 1880's and was presented at the court of St. James to Queen Victoria, who, it is said, later became a regular subscriber to the Solid Muldoon. Not a bad achievement for a man who was illiterate and couldn't sign his own name at the age of fourteen when he enlisted. In 1892, after thirteen years of publishing The Solid Muldoon in Ouray, he moved his paper to Durango and continued publishing under the name Durango Democrat, until his death in 1914.[10]

Ouray prospered and grew. The Uncompahgre Valley below the town supplied hay and feed for the thousands of horses and pack animals in the area and food stuffs for the miners, townspeople, and travelers. Ouray offered hotels, saloons, sporting ladies, merchants, livery stables, freighting companies, assay offices, health resorts, and good access to the richest mining region of the San Juans. A brickyard was constructed at the present day site of the swimming pool and a few brick buildings began to appear in the residential areas and on Main Street. During the early 1880's the first swimming pool, or plunge, was built at the Radium Springs Court on Fifth Street. Other pools followed, offering tub and shower baths. A sign in one early photograph proclaimed the following: "Radium Vapor Health Institute, Hot Vapor Cave Baths, Natural Massages — Rubs — Electric Treatments. Dr. C. V. Bates." Radium Springs Park, the site of the present swimming pool, has played a role in the changing Ouray scene. The warm springs area that was once a quagmire during the winter and impassable to freighters was the site of the First and Last Chance Saloon, flower gardens, the fish ponds, as well as the hanging tree used by vigilantes to execute a husband and wife who had starved, abused, and beaten to death a ten year old adopted girl. During the 1920's two small alligators were placed in a fenced, warm spring and they thrived for ten years. The swimming pool was built in the mid 1920's with hot water piped from a reliable source in the vicinity of Box Canyon. Radium Springs Park was also the site of Ouray's baseball park. Baseball became very popular at the turn of the century. Rivalry rapidly developed between the town teams of Telluride, Silverton, and Ouray, with the competition greatest between Silverton and Ouray. This became so keen that Ouray once hired a professional team from Montana and was the eventual winner of the season's series. The fans usually traveled between the two towns by carriage or horseback. However, one year Silverton ran special trains to Red Mountain and the passengers continued on by stage.

CHAPTER III

The Meeker Massacre in 1879 resulted in the eventual removal of the Utes in western Colorado to northeastern Utah in 1881. This intensified the development of the western slope. The Denver and Rio Grande reached Montrose in 1882 and it became the outfitting point for Ouray, Red Mountain, Telluride, and other camps of the southern San Juans. New silver ore discoveries were also being made in the Ironton and Red Mountain areas and the rich ore deposit at the Yankee Girl mine was discovered in the fall of 1882. Thousands rushed to the Red Mountain area to stake their claims and join the boom. It was quite obvious to the citizens of Ouray that a good wagon road connecting Ironton and Red Mountain, a distance of twelve miles, the first six of which were along Uncompahgre Canyon and its seemingly unsurmountable cliffs, was essential. Otto Mears agreed to build a toll road for controlling interest in the company in June 1883. He completed the Ouray and San Juan Toll road, his greatest toll road achievement, in September of the same year at an average cost of $10 thousand per mile.[11] His toll gate and hotel were located at Bear Creek Falls. Ouray became the most direct route to the mines of Red Mountain and the city prospered from the new mine activity. The Silverton merchants were dismayed for a time. The Denver and Rio Grande Railway had reached their town in 1882 from Durango, but would go no further. They did not have a good access road to Red Mountain, so they, too, contacted Otto Mears. He completed the Silverton to Red Mountain toll road, a distance of twelve miles, in November 1884. Ouray and Silverton were finally linked by wagon road. Freight rates decreased between both towns. The mines prospered and both cities thrived for the next ten years. The Ouray to Silverton toll road became famous.

The Ouray to Ironton section was named the Million Dollar or Chief Ouray Highway by later travelers during the 1920's. The total twenty-four mile length was often referred to as the Rainbow Route, Circle Route, and Otto Mears road. The first usage of the term "Million Dollar" for this stretch of road may have come into being when a stage coach passenger on an excursion from

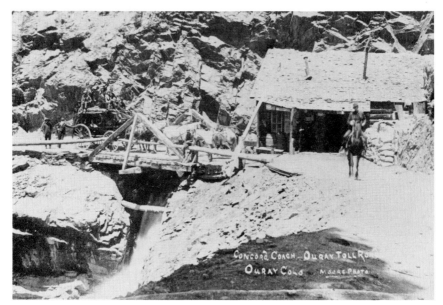

Concord coach-and-six at Mears toll gate and hotel located at Bear Creek Falls on Ouray and San Juan Toll Road. Note ore sacks stacked in front of hotel awaiting ore wagon from Ouray. *(Library, The State Historical Society of Colorado)*

Otto Mears toll road, Ouray to Silverton. *(Denver Public Library, Western History Department)*

the east bailed off the stage at the Bear Creek Falls toll gate and headed back to Ouray declaring all the time over his shoulder, "I wouldn't ride over that road again for a million dollars!"

Ore wagons piled high with supplies or loaded heavy with ore and their six head team of horses or mules, packers leading their pack string of mules single file down the street, burros being prodded ahead by their puncher, passengers climbing aboard stage coaches, and riderless horses trotting home to their stables, were all part of the everyday Ouray scene between the 1880's and 1910. The very life blood of Ouray and the mines was transportation. Clydesdale and Percheron horses were used to haul the heavy ore wagons. Pipe, mine rail, and timbers were tied to the pack saddle of the mules and burros with one end dragging the ground. Lumber was commonly cut longer than necessary as the average trail would take a foot off the length. Six horse teams, called "Big Sixes", were generally used to haul ore from the mines. The driver was called a teamster and he was the highest paid man in the trade, receiving $3.00 plus a meal at the mine for a days work of twelve to eighteen hours. During winter months sleighs were used with transfers made to wagons at lower elevations. The largest, richest and best equipped freighter on the western slope was Colorado's pioneer freighter, Dave Wood. His name was a household word during the 1880's. Unfortunately, the silver panic of 1893 was a personal financial disaster to him and he lost not only his silver mines, but his freight business, as well. John Ashenfelter was a local freighter hauling most of the ore from the mines in the Mt. Sneffels District. At one period alone, he had over thirty-two six-horse or mule teams hauling ore from, or machinery and supplies to, the mines in the district, over one hundred burros and mules used for packing, and a livery stable of fifty saddle horses for the miners to ride to the mines.[12] Ouray had several livery stables, all of which rented self-returning horses. Once a miner reached his destination, he tied the reins over the saddle horn and the animal promptly headed for town and its own stable. Accidents along the trails in summer and winter were commonplace. Snowslides were a constant threat to the winter traveler. The slides all had names and the native, then as now, was aware of their presence. The Mother Cline Slide and Riverside Slides were encountered between Bear Creek Falls and Ironton. The Waterhole Slide was on the Camp Bird mine road. The three crosses on the switchbacks north of Ironton were placed in memory of Reverend Martin Hudson and his two daughters, the 1963 victims of the East Riverside Slide.

Wagon loaded with sacks of high-grade from Camp Bird Mine - 1903. Taken at Uncompahgre Canyon bridge just out of town. *(Denver Public Library Western History Department)*

A big event in Ouray — arrival of the daily passenger train. Circle Route Stage's omnibus is parked at platform in rear. About 1918. *(Denver Public Library, Western History Department)*

With the completion of Mear's Ouray to Silverton toll roads, Ouray became more impatient for the coming of the railroad from Montrose. The Denver and Rio Grande built up the west side of the Uncompahgre River canyon from Ridgway and reached Ouray in 1887 after the residents had put up the $40 thousand requested by the railroad to defray expenses. Dave Day, the fiery editor, may have spurred the townspeople into final action by perpetrating a hoax. He appeared to purchase two farms four miles north of town. He advertised lots for sale to the settlers of his new town and pledged to pay for the spur to his town himself. Ouray knew the editor was capable of doing what he said. Remembering the Animas City and Durango incident, where the railroad ended its line a mile and a half short of Animas City and Durango, a new town was found, they promptly met the railroad's demands. The arrival of the railroad brought added prosperity to the mines and to Ouray. Freight rates dropped, the miners were able to mine lower grade ores and the silver mines thrived. Ouray continued as a trading and transportation center for the rich mining camps. Passenger service was initiated and travel to Salt Lake City or Denver became an easy matter.

Ouray's downtown section had begun to take on a new look and show a little class. The census of 1890 indicated that two thousand people lived in the community. Streets were being graded on a regular basis and boardwalks had appeared on Main Street. Ouray's first electric light plant was installed in 1885 and powered by water flumed or piped down from the Uncompahgre River to the power house. The magnificent Beaumont Hotel, one of the finest mountain resorts a traveler could visit, was completed in December 1886. Actual construction had taken less than a year and the cost reached $75 thousand, a substantial figure at that time. The hotel's furnishings had been purchased from the leading store in Chicago, Marshall Field. Mahogany furniture was used throughout. Chicago's own Palmer House had loaned its best trained staff members to assist in the grand opening. The Beaumont had a parlor, ballroom, saloon, and gameroom, the latest in kitchen facilities, and a spectacular dining room with walls and ceilings beautifully panelled in wood with a rosewood finish. The most remarkable featured may have been its rotunda that reached from the foyer to the cupola, an equivalent of four stories. The impressive grand stairway, with its two arms, ascended to the second floor. Balconies formed an open square around the rotunda on both the second and third floors. Glass front cases containing ore samples from the richest mines, and pictures of local scenery lined the walls of the foyer. The Circle

Beaumont Hotel lobby about 1920. The famous Beaumont clock seen in this picture is reported to have been recently stolen from the now closed hotel. *(Denver Public Library, Western History Department)*

LOBBY BEAUMONT HOTEL, OURAY, COLO.

X-1077

Beaumont Hotel lobby. Navajo blankets were used to decorate railing of second floor. *(Denver Public Library, Western History Department)*

A passenger-loaded Concord stagecoach in front of Beaumont Hotel. Probably enroute to Ironton and Red Mountain. *(Denver Public Library, Western History Department)*

Stage coach in front of Hotel Geneva, 1890's, with the snow covered peaks of the Amphitheater in the background. *(Library, The State Historical Society of Colorado)*

The St. Elmo as it originally looked upon completion in 1899. *(Denver Public Library, Western History Department)*

Mrs. Kittie Heit in front of Bon Ton Restaurant during construction of the St. Elmo Hotel to left of picture. 1898-1899. *(Denver Public Library, Western History Department)*

Route Stage left from in front of the Beaumont each day to travel the Rainbow Route to Red Mountain and Silverton. Ouray had several good hotels in the 1880's. The Dixon House, a two story frame structure, was a block east of Main near the City Hall and was the headquarters for the Barlow and Sanderson Stage Line. The Delmonica Hotel was completed in 1884 and stood on the now-vacant lot north of the Elks Lodge. Both the Dixon House and the Delmonica were later destroyed by fire. The three story Western Hotel, one of Ouray's better hotels for a number of years, was built by Holt & Foster in 1892 and was originally known by that name. The Western Hotel has beaten the odds in regard to fires. It is the largest, wooden structure remaining in Ouray and, although it has been the scene of three fires, none were serious enough to destroy it. Both the Beaumont and the Holt & Foster had special carriages to carry departing passengers to the train and to meet arrivals. The drivers would proclaim the merits of their respective hotels to arriving passengers and attempt to entice as many as possible on their carriage. The Geneva was another good hotel and it stood on the east side of Main Street between Seventh and Eighth. Mrs. Kittie Heit, who owned and operated the Bon Ton Restaurant, made enough money to build the St. Elmo next door in 1899. The St. Elmo is the only one of the early hotels still operating. The St. Elmo Hotel, Wright Building, Bon Ton Restaurant, and the Elks Lodge building across the street, narrowly escaped serious damage in the fall of 1909 when a cloudburst in the amphitheater sent voluminous quantities of water, mud, and rocks down Portland Creek, washing out bridges and cribbing. Fortunately, only a few buildings were destroyed, while others were filled with debris.

In 1888 the Ouray County Courthouse was built. The two story Wright's Hall was completed the same year. Wright's Hall was always called the "Opera House". The auditorium, complete with stage, was on the second floor and had a seating capacity of five hundred. Local theatrical groups and renown entertainers on the mine camp circuit performed here. The seats were removable, making it ideal for the Firemen's Annual Dance, as well as high school functions. The lower floor was occupied for many years by the San Juan Hardware Company. The Citizens State Bank occupies the old Office Building. Prevost's Corner Saloon was located on the first floor and the second floor was taken up with offices. The Orendorf Bakery, located across from the City Hall, had a delivery wagon that toured the town each day stocked with a full assortment of baked goods. The Ouray Lodge No. 492, B.P.O. Elks, the first lodge on the western slope of Colorado, was

The Beaumont Hotel showing stores lining the block to Sixth Ave. 1890's. *(Library, The State Historical Society of Colorado)*

Burros packed for the mountains. *(Library, The State Historical Society of Colorado)*

Dr. Rowan's drug store with post office in rear. The hard-to-see stuffed bear behind the key can be seen today in the Ouray Museum. *(Denver Public Library, Western History Department)*

Burros loaded with mine rail near Wright Building and Shillings Dry Goods Store.
(Library, The State Historical Society of Colorado)

Ouray and San Juan Toll Road around the 1890's. *(Denver Public Library, Western History Department*

organized in 1898. Dr. W. W. Rowan, the area's first doctor, who had a drug store on Main Street where the Ouray Cafe Bar now stands, was elected the first Exalted Ruler. The lodge building was constructed in 1904. The bar was originally from one of the saloons in Red Mountain.[13]

Riverside Slide below Ironton — probably slide of 1888. Riverside Tunnel 400 feet long and 40 feet high on Ouray and San Juan Toll Road. *(Denver Public Library, Western History Department)*

Bear Creek Trail to south of Ouray. *(Denver Public Library, Western History Department)*

Pack train of concentrates being taken from Camp Bird—King lease mine down to the Camp Bird mill above Ouray where it is transferred to ore wagons and carried to Ouray. These trails are over snow slides where the snow is often 40 feet deep. The mule skinners and pack trains are in constant danger of slides. In the spring when the soft snow at the side of the trail melts it leaves the hard packed trail standing above. If a mule steps off the trail into the soft snow, unless he lies perfectly still until it helped by the mule skinner, he will flounder and sink deep in the snow and smother to death. Horses are seldom used for this purpose because they invariably flounder in the snow if they step off the trail. *(Denver Public Library, Western History Department)*

The Western Hotel in 1942. The lobby and dining room is on the right and the bar on the left. A mug of 6% beer cost 10 cents. *(Denver Public Library, Western History Department)*

Bar in Western Hotel, May 1937. Domino cigarettes cost 10 cents a pack and you could buy two Town Talk cigars for a nickel. *(Denver Public Library, Western History Department)*

CHAPTER IV

Ouray offered a refreshing change of pace for the miner who came to town to see the bright lights on a Saturday night. After a hot mineral bath at any one of the several bath houses or barber shops, he had many choices for his evening's activities. Between the 1880's and the 1900's Ouray had as many as thirty saloons, big and small, operating simultaneously. A customer poured his own from a bottle and the usual cost of a drink was fifteen cents or two for a quarter. The Ouray Brewing Company was started in 1884 and for a few years it supplied a local product in draft and bottles. A half gallon of beer cost twenty-five cents. Some of the best meals in town were served in restaurants annexed to saloons. The Fritsch Brothers ran an excellent restaurant in the back room of Prevost's Corner Saloon.[14] At most restaurants and saloons meals could be obtained for twenty-five to fifty cents. Five dollar meal tickets offering thirty-five cent meals were sold at discount to attract business. Room and board was a dollar and a quarter per day or six to eight dollars by the week. Staying at the Beaumont was quite expensive and out of the question for most of the miners, as rooms alone cost three to four dollars a night.[15] Gambling was wide open and most of the saloons offered one or more games, such as faro, roulette, poker, and twenty-one. One of the saloons that didn't allow gambling was Theodore "Pat" Hess's, that occupied the corner of the Hess Building. Hess, a short, chunky German, decided to don the Green one St. Patrick's Day as a token of appreciation for his many Irish customers. A patron, in jest, called him "Pat". The name promptly stuck and soon everyone believed it was his true name.[16] The mining population was predominately Italian with the remainder being Irish and Swedish. John Vanoli's Roma was an early saloon in Ouray and very popular with the Italians. Several of the saloons had piano players to entertain the customers. The First and Last Chance Saloon north of town featured a country beer garden with benches and tables set in a grove of trees. Dance halls, featuring dance hall girl companionship, were popular at that time. A drink and a dance cost twenty-five cents with an extra fifteen cents for her drink. The girls received a percentage of the drinks and

Ouray's City Hall and Walsh Library prior to 1950 fire. *(Library, The State Historical Society of Colorado)*

dances they sold. The Gold Belt Theater and Dance Hall was located behind the present day Jim's Country Store. It had a stage where variety shows were presented in the early days. The corrugated covered building can be seen today, although it has been in disuse for many years. Ouray's red light district was located on Second Street between Seventh and Eighth, with both sides lined with cribs and parlor houses. About one hundred girls were on the line in establishments with titillating names such as: The Temple of Music, The Bird Cage, The Monte Carlo, The Clipper, Bon Ton, The Morning Star, and The Club.[17]

Ouray has always been proud of its Fourth of July celebrations. Sometimes as many as three excursion trains, each consisting of six or seven coaches, were used to bring celebrators from Grand Junction, Delta, and Montrose. In some years one or two trains came over from Telluride. Miners from the south and Silverton arrived by stage or horseback. It was the day for the firemen, miners, children, and spectators. One of the main events of the day was the drilling contest for the miners. These contests were held throughout the west and the champions of each mining district were eligible to compete in the national eliminations, where large purses were at stake. For weeks prior to the Fourth, the contestants had practiced improving their timing and steel changing. Contest steel had been sharpened and tempered by the best of the blacksmiths. New handles had been fixed to their favorite hammers. A block of uniform granite had been hauled to the park north of town and everything was in readiness. Betting became rampant on the Fourth, as each mine or camp supported his favorite. Wives and girl friends often taunted members of the opposing team by casting aspersions at their manhood. There were two events: single-jack contests for the individual driller and double-jack contests for two-man teams. The object was to drill the deepest hole in a given length of time, usually fifteen minutes. Perfect coordination, as well as strength, was required by the double-jack contestants. Drilling was done with one man kneeling, turning the steel in his hands and dripping water in the hole to wash out the rock dust. His partner, standing swinging the double-jack with both hands, maintained a steady tempo as he hit the steel. At a pre-arranged count, the kneeling man would grasp his double-jack with one hand and hit the steel while rising. At the same time, his partner, while assuming the kneeling position, would deliver a one-handed blow and grab the steel simultaneously. Both men could exchange places or change steel when longer lengths were required, without missing a stroke. Another big event was the water fight between opposing teams, some of

American Nettie Mine on Uncompahgre Canyon rim north of Ouray. 1800 foot tramway span to floor. This is a famous mine in the annals of American mining. Rich gold deposits being found in Dakota quartzite. *(Library, The State Historical Society of Colorado)*

Store and post office of Col. Porter at Sneffels, Colorado. 1880's. *(Library, The State Historical Society of Colorado)*

which were from neighboring towns. The water pressure in Ouray was enormous due to the height of the intake in the Uncompahgre canyon above the city. Unfortunately, small rocks were sometimes swept through the lines and men were seriously injured or blinded by the debris. Hose cart companies from nearby towns often competed in races.

Many pictures are still in existence of Ouray's parades. On July 3, 1897 the Ouray residents were greeted with several inches of snow. A twenty-five foot diameter, decorated arch had been placed in the center of Main just north of Sixth Avenue that year for the parade to pass under and evergreen trees had been cut and tied at the base of the power poles. For many years a large flagpole stood at the intersection of Sixth and Main. The extreme height of the pole is clearly evident in a picture taken during the 1890's, of the July Fourth parade line-up. Several Chinese had gathered at the Sam Pong Laundry. Spectators were lining up past the Beaumont Hotel and an army unit was patiently waiting for the parade to start. The Ouray Hose Cart Company and its members were in their harnesses and ready for the up-hill pull. Unions entered floats in the parade and in 1906 the Ouray Teamsters and Packers Union entered a flag-draped, canopied ore wagon with thirteen girls dressed in white, wearing colored sashes, each bearing the name of a prominent mine. The Munn Brothers Sampling Works building formed an appropriate backdrop to the team of Big Eights. The full dress uniforms of the volunteer firemen and their highly decorated hose and pump cart are shown in front of the City Hall in a picture taken the same year. Festivities were climaxed by a Roman Candle parade in which the children participated, and a fireworks display. Ouray's high society generally attended a formal ball at the Beaumont. The less socially-minded attended a more casual dance at Wright's Hall. Many of the miners preferred the boisterous atmosphere of the numerous saloons and dance halls.

Ouray, not unlike other towns in the Rocky Mountains, has always attracted tourists and photographers. Its picturesque location and economic importance to the San Juan area was acclaimed in Williams' 1877 Tourist Guide to the San Juan Mines of Colorado, less than one year after the town was incorporated. In 1885 Crofutt's Guide to Colorado extolled the medicinal merits of Ouray's hot springs and the grandeur of the amphitheater, comparing it to the coliseum of Rome. Visitors have enjoyed, for almost a century, the elk, deer, and Rocky Mountain sheep that occasionally graze within the city limits. A famous picture was taken in the 1930's of the elk grazing on the lawn in front of the

Ouray Teamsters and Packers Union entry for the July 4, 1906 parade. *(Denver Public Library, Western History Department)*

Concord coach-and-six in July Fourth parade, probably 1910. The Office Building with John Prevost's famous Corner Saloon in background. *(Denver Public Library, Western History Department)*

Fourth of July parade during the 1890's. *(Library, The State Historical Society of Colorado)*

Snow storm on July 3, 1897. *(Library, The State Historical Society of Colorado)*

Interior of Box Canyon, Ouray, Colorado. 1920's. *(Library, The State Historical Society of Colorado)*

Ouray flood scene. Portland Creek flume next to St. Elmo Hotel. Mrs. Kittie Heit owned the St. Elmo, as well as the Elks Boarding House at the far left of the picture.
(Denver Public Library, Western History Department)

Visiting Elks from the Amphitheater, at the Ouray Lodge.   *(Ouray Lodge No. 492 B.P.O.E. Elks. Photo by Beverly Spencer)*

Upper Camp Bird installation. Also known as Camp Bird South. *(Library, The State Historical Society of Colorado)*

Elks Lodge. The entrance to Box Canyon was blasted out by the power company in the late 1890's for a water line. For the first time, sightseers were able to enter the narrow, perpendicular canyon formed by the waters of Canyon Creek cutting down through solid rock, and view the water fall as it plunges to the canyon floor with a deafening roar. A special attraction for the spring and early summer tourist is the well-named Cascade Falls east of town. Early tours were made to Bear Creek Falls where the tourists enjoyed the falls, mountains, and sheer canyon scenery. The dangerous roads took their toll of tourists, as well as of natives. The July 22, 1897 edition of the Dolores Star notes the death of a young girl from Illinois, which occurred on a YMCA excursion when the carriage in which she was riding overturned when the horse became frightened on the road near Bear Creek Falls. With the completion of Otto Mears' Silverton Railroad to the Red Mountain area in 1888, tourists came to ride the Rainbow Route to Red Mountain or Ironton and the connecting stage coach to Ouray. The Denver and Rio Grande Railroad was promoting its Around the Circle trips which ran from Salida through Durango to Silverton, and from Ouray returning to Salida via the Black Canyon and Gunnison. The Silverton Railroad and the Bear Creek Falls toll road were the connecting link. Fliers were forwarded to travel agents throughout the nation and the Circle Trip became a popular tourist attraction. The Rio Grande ads praised the scenery along the Rainbow Route and the eight and one-half mile daylight ride in Concord coaches through the Uncompahgre Canyon from Ironton to Ouray.[18]

CHAPTER V

In the 1890's there occurred an event that ended the silver boom, devastated the empires of the silver barons, and nearly emptied many of the towns and mining camps of the San Juans; this was known as the Silver Panic of 1893. As early as 1873, the silver mines had been subject to falling prices. In that year the United States, like many of the European nations, abandoned the bi-metal standard that had established the coining of gold and silver in the ratio of sixteen silver to one gold, and adopted an exclusive gold standard. Silver was without a base for the first time and the price declined, due partially to the added production thrown on the market from the new-found mines in the Colorado Rockies. The silver interests failed in their attempt to re-establish the old sixteen-to-one bi-metal ratio. However, the Bland-Allison Act of 1878 provided for congress to purchase between two and four million dollars worth of silver each month. Prices rallied briefly and reached $1.21 an ounce, 8 cents lower than the high in 1873, and then continued their gradual decline.[19] The silver operators knew that many mines would be forced to shut down when the price declined to $1 an ounce. They also knew that if the price "continued to slide below 80 cents, mass shutdowns would occur with catastrophic results for all".[20] In 1890 the Sherman Silver Purchase Act was passed and it guaranteed that the U.S. Treasury would purchase 4.5 million ounces of silver each month, the approximate total mine production at that time. This was almost double the amount purchased under the previous act. During 1889 prices had rallied from 95 cents to $1.05, the price at the time of the passage of the Sherman Silver Act. This latest bill helped maintain prices only momentarily, then they continued to decline even more steeply than before. Grover Cleveland, the foe of western silver and the friend of the eastern gold interests who were afraid of declining gold prices, was nominated and elected president of the United States in 1892. By the spring of 1893 an epidemic of business and bank failures had swept the country. In addition, silver prices were decreasing at the same time that the recent discoveries in Creede were increasing their output. Prices

Sneffels store and post office. Ore sacks on dock await shipment to Ouray. *(Denver Public Library, Western History Department)*

Part of north end of store and post office at Sneffels. Posters advertise Lester Allens Big Minstrels. *(Denver Public Library, Western History Department)*

Yankee Girl Mine, March 27, 1891. Engine No. 100 (Ouray) on the lead track of the Yankee Girl — also referred to as Red Mountain Switch by some old timers. *(Library, State Historical Society of Colorado. Photo by White, Ouray)*

Silverton Railroad above Chattanooga. Train enroute to Red Mountain and Ironton. *(Denver Public Library, Western History Department. Photo by McKee)*

The north end of Red Mountain during winter of 1891-1892. On August 20, 1892 fire started in the Red Mountain Hotel, 2 story building with occupants standing on balcony, and 14 buildings including all those pictured were burned to the ground. Red Mountain never recovered. *(Denver Public Library, Western History Department)*

An 1889 Main Street scene in Ironton looking north toward the end of Silverton Railway line — The Albany Mine. The famous Strayer Hotel is the building behind the bicyclist's hat. *(Library, The State Historical Society of Colorado)*

Famous Silverton Railroad turntable in Corkscrew Gulch, June 1889. Right track goes to Ironton and Albany Mine. Left track proceeds to Guston, Yankee Girl, Red Mountain, and Silverton. *(Denver Public Library, Western History Department)*

continued their decline, fell to 87 cents and by mid-1893 hit 78 cents. President Cleveland asked for repeal of the Sherman Silver Purchase Act in late June. The price was 63 cents. By mid-summer hundreds of miners, at an ever-increasing rate, were leaving the prospects and mines. Otto Mears' railroad, The Rio Grande Southern, running between Durango, Rico, Telluride, and Ridgway, which was completed in December 1891, went into receivership on August 2.[21] The financial panic continued. A long filibuster delayed voting in the Senate. On October 30, 1893 the Sherman Silver Purchase Act was repealed and government silver purchases ended that day. The telegraphs sent the news out to all western mining camps within seconds. Within minutes the price of silver hit 50 cents.[22]

After the Silver Panic of 1893 the businesses of Ouray went into a mild recession that lasted the next three years. Unlike many of the silver camps of Colorado, several of the mines in the Ouray area contained sufficient gold to make their mining profitable. These mines continued to operate while prospectors searched for new properties carrying high gold values.

The principal mining areas that are tributary to Ouray can be grouped, due to their isolation, into three districts, all within twelve miles of Ouray: The Uncompahgre, Red Mountain, and Mt. Sneffels Districts. The mines immediately north of Ouray along the east side of the valley were in the Uncompahgre District. The Calliope lead-silver ore body was discovered in 1887. The rich silver ore of the adjoining Bachelor Lode was not discovered until 1892. The extraordinarily rich American Nettie gold deposit was discovered in 1889. Other mines to the south and east of Ouray, practically within hailing distance of town, were also included in this district. The mines in the Uncompahgre District were totally dependent upon Ouray for all their necessities, including transportation and manpower. Production continued for a few years and the mines gradually closed due to high operating costs, low prices, and the apparent lack of ore bodies with sufficient tonnages to support a sustained operation.

In 1881 the phenomenal silver ore deposits between Red Mountain and Ironton were discovered in the Red Mountain District, some twelve miles south of the city. The Yankee Girl and Guston Mines were opened in 1882, followed by the National Bell in 1883. The activity of Red Mountain and Ironton, thriving communities of some 1000 people, continued to increase until 1893 when the boom collapsed due to falling silver prices and lower grade ores being encountered at depth. The ores from Red Mountain District were initially transported by pack team, and later by wagon, to

Boarding House at the upper level of Virginius Mine. Elevation 12,500 feet. *(Library, The State Historical Society of Colorado)*

Virginius Basin showing three main working levels of the Virginius Mine. The elevation of the Basin is 12,000 feet with the high peak in the center exceeding 13,300 feet. *(Library, The State Historical Society of Colorado)*

Silverton for smelting or further shipment by the Denver and Rio Grande Railway to the smelter in Durango. In 1888 the Silverton Railroad, built by Otto Mears, reached Red Mountain and Ironton. This unique rail system, with its Corkscrew Gulch turntable on the main line, had a reputation of being the steepest (5% grade), the crookedest (30 degree curves), and the most profitable in Colorado.[23] Freight rates were reduced and the mines were able to ship lower grade ores, thus extending the life of the existing mines and enabling the miners to open up new ones. The entire north end of Red Mountain had been devastated by a fire that destroyed fifteen buildings in August of 1892. With the falling silver prices during 1893, the town never again reached its former stature. The Guston and Yankee Girl Mines continued to operate until 1896, when they finally shut down because of low prices and increased mining costs, due partially to the corrosive action of the mine waters. The Joker Tunnel, a drainage and access tunnel driven below the mine workings of the Guston and Yankee Girl Mines in 1906, resulted in comparatively little production. Because of the Silverton oriented railroad facilities, the mines in the Red Mountain District were more dependent on that city as a center of commerce, than they were on Ouray. The only mining activity of any consequence in this district today, is the Idarado Mining Company's operation at the Treasury Tunnel. The 3.5 mile tunnel was driven through the mountain to the Telluride side during WW II to intersect the Black Bear and other veins. The mining division has its offices and facilities on the Red Mountain side and the milling division mills the ore on the Telluride side. The Idarado Mining Company is the largest, single employer in Ouray County.

The district whose mines played the greatest role in the development and prosperity of Ouray was the Mt. Sneffels District, some eight miles southwest and 1500 to 4800 feet higher in elevation. Because of its inaccessibility, this might appear to be an unlikely prospect, as the trails were often blocked with falling rocks in summer and avalanches in the winter. Deep snow slides blocking a road were often tunneled through with an opening large enough to accommodate ore wagons and stage coaches.

One of the first mines to be developed was the Virginius, located high on the rocky slopes of Virginius Basin at an elevation of 12,500 feet. By 1881 this mine, from its snow and wind-swept, alpine perch, had produced 75 thousand dollars worth of silver ore through two shafts and three levels.[24] Ore was packed and freighted to the nearest railroad for shipment to the Hill Works in Denver, or packed to the Windham Smelter north of Ouray, a

Col. Porter's store and post office at Porter, later Sneffels, Colorado. Taking out remains of the victims killed in Virginius Snowslide, probably slide of January 3, 1884. *(Library, The State Historical Society of Colorado)*

tedious and expensive process.[25] The Virginius continued operations from its mountain top site until around 1895, when the last
ore was shipped from the upper workings. The Revenue tunnel
was completed about 1893 and by 1896 all ore was removed
through the tunnel whose portal location was on Canyon Creek.[26]
This 7500 foot tunnel intersected the Virginius vein at an elevation of 10,800 feet, some 2000 feet below its surface outcrop, and
was directly responsible for mining operations being profitably
continued for the next twenty years. More than one hundred miners lived in the bunkhouses at Virginius Basin while working at
the Virginius. Snow slides were commonplace and a constant
threat to the buildings and their occupants during the winter and
spring months. The winter of 1884 was especially severe and the
resulting snow slides took hundreds of lives in the San Juans. One
serious slide swept down from the rocky crags above the mine on
January 3, 1884, killing four miners instantly and seriously injur-
ing a dozen more.[27] To help reduce damage from such slides,
buildings were often built right up against the walls of the basin
with a reinforced, steep-pitched roof in an attempt to project the
movement of the slide over and away from the structure and its
occupants. Pack trains arrived almost daily with supplies from
Ouray, and returned laden with sacks of ore. It required ten burros or seven mules to carry a ton of ore, a wagon being capable of
hauling from two to four tons. The store and post office was
moved to Porter, later named Sneffels, the town built near the
portal of the tunnel. The Revenue Tunnel was one of the first
mines to use electricity. The ore train was powered by electric
locomotives, the tunnel and stations were lit with electric lights,
and the mill was powered electrically. The tunnel was driven for
drainage, ventilation, and for access to the veins. As many as
600 men were employed mining and milling the ore from the
Virginius and other veins that were intersected at depth. The
town of Sneffels became the headquarters for the district. During
the height of the boom, it is believed that as many as 3000 people
worked in the Mt. Sneffels District. Sneffels became a thriving
community and prospered for almost thirty years. A few former
residents return to Ouray each year to seek out old friends and
make another trip to the canyon that was the center of so much
activity seventy years ago.

The most famous mine in the Sneffels District is the Camp
Bird, discovered by Thomas Walsh, who later purchased the Star
of the East diamond for his daughter, Evalyn. He had a home in
Ouray and was generous in his support of the town. He donated
funds in 1902 for the library, bell, and clock, all of which were

Sneffels skiiers on a trip to the store. *(Library, The State Historical Society of Colorado)*

Sneffels looking east to Virginius-Revenue tunnel mill. Jan. 1897. *(Library, State Historical Society of Colorado)*

destroyed when the City Hall burned in 1950. His daughter is probably best remembered for her ownership of the Hope diamond, which she purchased after he died.[28] Ouray's prosperity, now as in the past, is closely tied to the Camp Bird Mine. Thomas Walsh, operator of the Silverton smelter treating low grade silver ore from the Guston Mine, had lost most of his money in the panic and was approaching bankruptcy. He is credited with the discovery of high grade gold ore in 1896 on the Una and Gertrude claims, two deserted silver-lead mines in Imogene Basin. The same year he purchased the two claims for $10 thousand and staked an additional claim next to the Gertrude that he named the Camp Bird.[29]

He soon gained control of practically all the properties in the basin and the consolidation of his holdings became known as the Camp Bird. A mill was built at the mouth of Virginius Basin and a connecting two-mile aerial tram was completed to the mine. By 1899 the Camp Bird had been opened up extensively with almost a mile of underground workings. Ore below $10 in value was not mined. The material, ore and waste rock removed by driving the main tunnel alone, contained enough gold in places to assay $1600 per linear foot.[30] Between 1896 and 1902, the year the mine was sold to a British syndicate for $6 million, of which $3.5 million was in cash, the mine had produced about 700 thousand dollars worth of ore annually.[31] It was a fabulous mine and by 1916 the total value of ores mined exceeded $27 million. Near the mine entrance, at some 11,200 feet in elevation, he built his three story boarding house in 1899 to accommodate 400 miners. It was the finest that money could buy and equipped with a reading room, game room, and a store that stocked any item a miner might request. The building was lighted with electricity, heated with steam, equipped with flush toilets, hot and cold running water, porcelain bath tubs, and marble-topped wash basins. The miners ate in the dining room, off china dishes instead of the usual tinware. Snow slides took their toll of the San Juan intruders and the boarding house was soon destroyed and later rebuilt along identical lines.

1893 marked the beginning of the use of aerial trams to transport ore, and the long distance transmission of alternating current for power. In 1897 the Telluride Power Transmission Company transmitted power seventeen miles to the Camp Bird Mine, the longest distance electric power had ever been transmitted in the United States.[32] With the exception of a few years, 1916-1926, the mine has been in continuous operation since 1896. The Camp Bird operates today from a lower tunnel driven near the mill.

1888 Riverside Slide and tunnel between Bear Creek Falls and Ironton. *(Denver Public Library, Western History Department. Photo by McKee)*

Ore wagons picking up sacks of ore at Camp Bird Mine. 1903. *(Denver Public Library, Western History Department. Photo by G. L. Bean)*

Tramway at Camp Bird Mine. Throughout the rugged San Juan Mountains, this was the accepted manner in which miners traveled to and from work. Early 1900's.

(Library, The State Historical Society of Colorado)

Chief Ouray, chief of the Uncompahgre or Tabeguache Utes. Born 1833, died August 24, 1880. *(Library. The State Historical Society of Colorado)*

During the early productive years, and ending in 1926, all supplies and ore shipments were hauled from Ouray by pack trains or six-horse teams over the narrow, steep, crooked mountain roads. Perhaps the best description of the Camp Bird's importance lies buried in J. D. Irving's statement concerning Ouray in 1904:

> "The town of Ouray, Colorado, long an important mining center, now chiefly known as the place from which one may most readily reach the Camp Bird mine, is located ..."[33]

Camp Bird Mill showing staff buildings and offices. Taken around 1912. *(Library, The State Historical Society of Colorado. Photo by McClure, Denver)*

Early picture of Bear Creek Falls. *(Denver Public Library, Western History Department)*

FOOTNOTES

1. William S. Wallace, Antoine Robidoux 1794-1860, 1953, pp. 1, 14-19.
2. Sidney Jocknick, Early Days on the Western Slope of Colorado, 1913, (1968), p. 123.
3. Frank A. Rice, History of Ouray, Original Manuscript in Walsh Library, Ouray, Colorado, 1958, 1961, p. 3.
4. Muriel S. Wolle, Stampede to Timberline, 1949, p. 380.
5. Morris F. Taylor, The Barlow and Sanderson Stage Lines in Colorado, 1872-1884, The Colorado Magazine, L/2, 1973, pp. 142-162.
6. Ray Cooper, "Cooper's History", The Silverton Standard and the Miner, March 3 - April 7, 1939, (June 14, 1974).
7. George A. Crofutt, Crofutt's Grip Sack Guide of Colorado, Vol. II-1885, 1885, (1966), p. 162.
8. Helen M. Searcy, Col. Dave Day, Pioneers of the San Juan Country, 1942, p. 77.
9. William Rathmell, History of Ouray, Original Manuscript in Walsh Library, Ouray, Colorado, p. 33.
10. Helen M. Searcy, op cit pp. 76-80.
11. Michael D. Kaplin, The Toll Road Building Career of Otto Mears, 1881-1887, The Colorado Magazine, LII/2, 1975, p. 162.
12. Frank A. Rice, op cit, p. 35.
13. ibid, pp. 44-51.
14. ibid, p. 61.
15. Ouray Plaindealer, January 9, 1890.
16. Frank A. Rice, op cit, p. 62.
17. Wilson Rockwell, Uncompahgre Country, 1965, p. 236.
18. Robert Sloan, Carl A. Skowronski, The Rainbow Route, 1975, p. 124.
19. John W. Vanderwilt, Metals, Non Metals and Fuels, Mineral Resources of Colorado, 1947, p. 20.
20. Phyllis F. Dorset, The New Eldorado, 1970, p. 337.
21. Mallory H. Ferrell, Silver San Juan, 1973, p. 88.
22. Phyllis F. Dorset, op cit, p. 344.
23. Robert E. Sloan, Carl A. Skowronski, op cit, p. 56.
24. Chester W. Purlington, Preliminary Report on the Mining Industries of the Telluride Quandrangle, Colorado. 18th Annual Report, U.S.G.S. Pt III, 1898, p. 836.
25. Ervan F. Kushner, A Guide to Mineral Collecting at Ouray Colorado, 1973, p. 44.
26. Chester W. Purlington, op cit, p. 836.
27. Rocky Mountain News, January 3, 1884, p. 3.
28. Evalyn Walsh McLean, Father Struck it Rich, 1936, p. 191.

29. Frederick L. Ransome, Economic Geology of the Silverton Quadrangle, Colorado, U.S.G.S. B. 182, 1901 p. 24.
30. ibid, p. 202.
31. Charles W. Henderson, Mining in Colorado, U.S.G.S. PP. 138, 1926, p. 185.
32. ibid, p. 12.
33. John D. Irving, Ore Deposits of the Ouray District, U.S.G.S. B. 260, 1905, p. 50.

BIBLIOGRAPHY

BOOKS

CROFUTT, GEORGE A. Crofutt's Grip Sack Guide of Colorado, Vol. II, 1885. Omaha, Overland Publishing Co., CUBAR Reprint, 1966.

D.A.R., SARAH PLATT DECKER CHAPTER. Pioneers of the San Juan Country, Vols. I-IV. Colorado Springs, Outwest Printing and Stationery, 1969.

DORSET, PHYLLIS F. The New Eldorado. New York, The Macmillan Co., 1970.

FERRELL, MALLOY H. Silver San Juan. Boulder, Pruett Publishing Co., 1973.

HAFEN, LE ROY R. AND ANN W. Old Spanish Trail. Glendale, Calif., Arthur H. Clark Co., 1954.

HENDERSON, CHARLES W. Mining in Colorado. U.S.G.S. P.P. 610, 1926.

IRVING, JOHN D. Ore Deposits of the Ouray District. U.S.G.S. B260, 1905.

JEFFERSON J., DELANEY R., THOMPSON G. The Southern Utes, Ignatio, Colorado, Southern Ute Tribe, 1972.

JOCKNICK, SIDNEY. Early Days on the Western Slope of Colorado. Glorieta, N.M., Rio Grande Press, Inc., 1913 Reprint, 1968.

KAPLAN, MICHAEL D. The Toll Road Building Career of Otto Mears, 1881-1887. The Colorado Magazine, LII/2, 1975.

KUSHNER, ERVAN F. A guide to Mineral Collecting at Ouray, Colorado, Second Edition. Paterson, N.J., 1973.

LAVENDER, DAVID. The Big Divide. Garden City, N.Y., Doubleday & Co., Inc., 1949.

McLEAN, EVALYN W. Father Struck it Rich. Boston, Little, Brown, and Co., 1936.

PURLINGTON, CHESTER W. Preliminary Report on the Mining Industries of the Telluride Quadrangle, Colorado, 18th Annual Report, U.S.G.S. Pt. III, 1898.

RANSOME, FREDERICK L. Economic Geology of the Silverton Quadrangle, Colorado, U.S.G.S. B182, 1901.

RATHMELL, WILLIAM. History of Ouray. Unpublished manuscript in Walsh Public Library, Ouray, Colorado, undated.

RICE, FRANK A. History of Ouray. Unpublished manuscript in Walsh Public Library, Ouray, Colorado, 1958, 1961.

ROCKWELL, WILSON. Uncompahgre Country. Denver, Sage Books, 1967.

SLOAN AND SKOWRONSKI, ROBERT E. AND CARL A. The Rainbow Route. Denver, Sundance, Ltd., 1975

SLOANE, HOWARD N. AND LUCILLE L. A pictorial History of American Mining. New York, Crown Publishers, Inc., 1970.

TAYLOR, MORRIS F. The Barlow and Sanderson Stage Lines in Colorado, 1872-1884. The Colorado Magazine, L/2, 1973.

VANDENBUSCHE, DUANE. Early Days in the Gunnison Country. Gunnison, Vandenbusche Books, 1974.

VANDERWILT, JOHN W. Mineral Resources of Colorado. Denver, State Mineral Resources Board, 1947.

WALLACE, WILLIAM S. Antoine Robidoux, 1749-1860. Los Angeles, Glen Dawson, 1953.

WILLIAMS. Tourist Guide to the San Juan Mines, 1877. Golden, Colorado, CUBAR Reprint, 1965.

WOLLE, MURIEL S. Stampede to Timberline. Chicago, Sage Books, 1949.

NEWSPAPERS

The Silverton Standard and The Miner.
The Dolores Star Diamond Jubilee, 1897-1971.
The Solid Muldoon.
Rocky Mountain News, January 3, 1884.
Ouray Plaindealer.

THE SILVERY SAN JUAN

Wherever I wander, my spirit still dwells,
In the silvery San Juan with its streamlets and dells;
Whose mountainous summits, so rugged and high,
With their pinnacles pierce the ethereal sky;
Where the daisy, the rose, and the sweet columbine
Blend their colors with those of the sober hued pine;
Where the ceaseless erosions of measureless time,
Have chiseled the grotto and canon sublime;
Have sculptured the cliff, and the stern mountain wall;
Have formed the bold turret, impressive and tall;
Have cut the deep gorge with its wonderful caves,
Sepulchral and gloomy; whose vast architraves
Support the stalactites, both pendant and white,
Which with the stalagmites beneath them unite;
Where nestles a valley, sequestered and grand,
Worn out of the rock by the same tireless hand,
Surrounded by mountains, majestic and gray,
Which smile from their heights on the Town of Ouray.

* * * * * * * *

Wherever I wander, my ears hear the sound
Of thy waters, which plunge with a turbulent bound
O'er the precipice, seething and laden with foam;
My ears hear their music wherever I roam;
Where the cataract's rhapsody, joyous and light,
Enchants in the morning and soothes in the night;
Where blend the loud thunders, sonorous and deep,
With the whispering zephyr, and murmuring breeze,
Unite with the soft, listless sigh of the trees;
And where to the fancy, the voices of air
Wail in tones of distress, or in shrieks of despair;
Where mourneth the night wind, with desolate breath,
In accents suggestive of sorrow and death;
As falls from the heavens, so fleecy and light,
The winter's immaculate mantle of white;
Wherever I wander, these sounds greet my ears,
And the silvery San Juan to my fancy appears.

By Alfred Castner King